The Economic Stagnation of the Black Middle Class

A Briefing Before
The United States Commission on Civil Rights
Held in Washington, D.C., July 15, 2005

I0430286

Briefing Report

Table of Contents

Executive Summary..1

Evidence and Explanation of the Economic Stagnation of the Black Middle Class (Relative to Whites)
Douglas J. Besharov..7

Expanding the African-American Middle Class: Improving Labor Market Outcomes
Harry J. Holzer..16

The Black Middle Class: Growth or Decline?
Bart Landry..21

Statement of Chairman *Gerald A. Reynolds* on The Stagnation of the Black Middle Class......28

Statement of Commissioner *Michael J. Yaki* on The Stagnation of the Black Middle Class......30

Speaker Biographies..31

Executive Summary

On July 15, 2005, a panel of experts briefed members of the U.S. Commission on Civil Rights on explanations for and consequences of stagnation in the growth of America's black middle class. Professor Douglas Besharov from the University of Maryland School of Public Affairs and Senior Scholar at the American Enterprise Institute led the discussion. Dr. Harry Holzer, Professor of Public Policy, Georgetown Public Policy Institute, and Dr. Bart Landry, Professor of Sociology, University of Maryland, College Park and author of THE NEW BLACK MIDDLE CLASS, also made presentations and offered their expertise. The briefing was held in Room 2226 of the Rayburn House Office Building in Washington, D.C., and was televised by C-SPAN.

A transcript of the briefing is available on the Commission's website, www.usccr.gov, and by request from Publications Office, U.S. Commission on Civil Rights, 624 Ninth Street, NW, Room 600, Washington, D.C. 20425, (202) 376-8128, publications@usccr.gov.

Professor Douglas Besharov

Professor Besharov argues that while the African-American middle class is growing in absolute terms, it is not growing as a percentage of the African-American population. His data indicate that African-Americans were twice as likely to be in the lowest income decile, but also show that people earning more than $87,000 increased by 66 percent during that time. According to data he collected from a variety of sources, African-Americans were catching up to whites in both the top two quintiles and the top three quintiles until 1980, after which the percentage of African-Americans in the middle class has stayed constant.

Besharov believes that discrimination is not as significant a factor in explaining the stagnation as it once was. Rather, he cites the two following causes as large contributing factors:

- *Educational Attainment*: Professor Besharov cites educational attainment as the main proximate cause for the stagnation. According to data cited by Besharov, there has been a 30-year rise in high school completion, college attendance, and college graduation rates by African-Americans. However, he also points to an increase in the college dropout rate. The African-American male college graduation rate is 18 percent compared to 31 percent for white males.

- *Family structure*: Married-couple families tend to have higher incomes than female-headed families. According to data he presented, African-Americans are less likely to be in married-couple families.

- *Government employment*: Government employment was an important element of African-American progress as a source of non-discriminatory employment. However, public sector incomes have not kept pace with those in the private sector.

1

Finally, he cites the differences in *educational attainment*

Besharov attributes the differences in educational attainment to:

- *Poor high school counseling*, whereby high school counselors recommend students attend colleges for which they are not academically prepared.
- *Unsupportive college cultures* for those from disadvantaged backgrounds.
- *Financial aid formulas tilted in favor of the middle class*, rather than directed to low-income families and students.

Besharov recommends better college counseling at the high school level, so that students are matched up with colleges for which they are academically prepared. The evidence he cites, specifically Richard H. Sander, *A Systematic Analysis of Affirmative Action in American Law Schools*, 57 STANFORD LAW REVIEW 367 (2004), indicates that many young people attend colleges and graduate schools for which they are not academically prepared. The resulting "mismatch" between the student's qualifications and the academic rigor of the school helps explain poor performance in college and high dropout rates in general. Professor Besharov argues that African-American graduation rates would rise if there were a better match between the incoming students' academic achievement and the school's level of academic rigor.

Furthermore, he recommends that higher education financial aid programs and policies take into account families' wealth and assets, including home ownership, so that financial aid becomes more available to low-income students, rather than a middle class entitlement program.

Dr. Harry J. Holzer

Dr. Holzer ties the stagnation to changes in the labor market for Americans with different levels of educational attainment in that time period. According to Dr. Holzer, data from the Census Bureau's Current Population Survey suggest that employment and earnings are strongly related to educational attainment for all ethnic groups, that African-American males men lag significantly behind white males in earnings (20 to 25 percent) and employment, with largest gaps present at lower levels of educational attainment, and that the average earnings of individual black workers with some college education are sufficient to attain middle class status. Conversely, those with only a high school education require two earners in a household to attain that status.

Overall, he attributes much of these gaps to lack of early work experience, persistent discrimination, weak informal career networks among African-Americans, and geographic mismatches between jobs and workers. He also indicates that, while the 1990s saw positive employment trends for African-American women thanks in part to welfare reform and the growth in work supports like the Earned Income Tax Credit, the same period saw a continuing decline in work activity for less-educated African-American males. Holzer states that the incarceration rates of African-American males (1/3 of that population is under the supervision of the criminal justice system) relative to other groups and the growth in child support enforcement severely limit their prospects in accessing and staying in the labor market.

Holzer proposes several reforms to help increase access to the labor market for African-Americans:

- *Closing the achievement gap*, including occupational training, work experience, and apprenticeship as part of wide range of curricular reform efforts;
- *The use of career academies and community colleges*, which have shown positive impacts on the earnings and access to the middle access for the disadvantaged. Specifcally, he cites evidence that career academies link young African-American males to the labor market and give them early work experience, both leading to more long-term rational employment decisions on their part.
- *The use of labor market intermediaries*, such as temp agencies
- *Preventing early fatherhood*
- *Improving efforts to re-integrate ex-offenders into society and re-enter the labor market*, such as less strict child support laws.

Dr. Bart Landry

Citing his 1987 work, *The New Black Middle Class*, Landry states that the African-American middle class emerged in the early twentieth century and increased dramatically after the Civil Rights Act of 1964. This growth continued into the 1970s, 1980s, and 1990s, in part because of enforcement of anti-discrimination laws in employment. While he notes that the gap between the overall sizes of the African-American and white middle classes has declined substantially, he cites statistics that indicated that a higher proportion of whites than African-Americans has been clustered in the upper middle class since 1983.

Drawing from the Weberian sociological tradition, Dr. Landry posits a two-stage process of class mobility. First, in the period of life extending to age 21 or 22, we acquire skills that will prepare us to enter the labor market. Second, we barter or exchange these skills for jobs in the manual or non-manual sector of the labor market. The non-manual sector is often associated with middle class status. Those who do not attend college are limited to bartering in manual or unskilled service, while those with a college education barter in the non-manual sector. There are economic resources attached to positions in these sectors, namely income, fringe benefits, mobility opportunities, and job security.

The resources attached to these positions provide a starting point for future generations. According to Dr. Landry, the future economic fortunes of children depend on the economic resources and "cultural capital" of the family into which a child is born. Parents with a college education may understand the educational system better than those without and therefore can negotiate with colleges on their child's behalf.

Consequently, he argues, children from working class and low-income backgrounds are more likely to be placed into lower track classes, placed into less rigorous schools, and be less college-prepared. As a result, they are less able to compete for middle class occupations. Worse, Dr. Landry argues, the process is cumulative—each generation begins the process with the financial and educational resources accumulated or not accumulated in the past. Therefore, he recommends that schools provide the extra resources to provide these children with a quality education and facilitate upward mobility.

Landry pointed to recent high profile class action employment discrimination suits won by women working on Wall Street, as well as others in housing, mortgage lending, and employment, as evidence of intense discrimination. He recommended continued vigorous enforcement of affirmative action, even for those who had reached the middle class.

Discussion

Chairman Gerald A. Reynolds notes that he found a discussion on the role of culture lacking in the presentations. He discussed an exchange he had with a Washington, D.C. school principal about how peer cultural biases against academic achievement act as a barrier to that achievement. Specifically, the Chairman cites stories of young African-American male students being harassed in their neighborhoods if they carried books home from school.

Vice Chair Abigail Thernstrom follows these remarks by asking Dr. Holzer whether it would be useful to present data showing the relationship between earnings and cognitive skills would be more useful than simply analyzing educational attainment, since that might simply indicate time spent in school. Dr. Holzer agrees that such data would be useful, but that educational attainment is a more useful starting point for analyzing the labor problem, since this is the first thing employers look for.

Professor Besharov responds to Chairman Reynolds' comments about culture with what he saw as positive cultural trends with respect to ending the stagnation, namely a 30-percent decline in the out-of-wedlock birth rate among African-Americans. He also mentions the importance of the cultural role played by leaders and mediating institutions like churches in enforcing a positive view of education and family responsibility in the African-American community. Chairman Reynolds agrees that community leaders had a role to play in enforcing this view of education. He adds that family structure and a supportive home environment were key determinants in a child's academic success.

Dr. Landry responds to Chairman Reynolds' comments about culture by citing a recent study that concluded that African-American children do not conceal academic achievement or aspirations. He also cites research that indicated that African-American students adjusted their academic aspirations, which often exceeded those of their white peers, downward as a rational response to their unique economic obstacles.

Commissioner Jennifer Braceras asks what disaggregation of labor market and educational data concerning different ethnic groups and immigrant groups demonstrated. Dr. Holzer responds that this disaggregation indicated that immigrants work at much higher rates than native-born African-American males. He cites immigrant networks that generate employment opportunities as one explanation for this difference. Dr. Landry attributes the higher work rates among immigrants to their alleged greater willingness to accept unfair or unsafe labor conditions. Besharov adds that statistically comparing educational attainment between native-born Hispanics and immigrant Hispanics tells a different story, namely that the statistics for high school graduation of native-born Hispanics are comparable to whites and African-Americans.

Commissioner Michael Yaki asks if examining education and wealth and capital accumulation is the only way to examine the stagnation issue, since the issue affects many who had already completed their education. Dr. Holzer agrees that access to better paying jobs for those already in the work force and traditional civil rights issues remained on the table. Professor Besharov counters that education should remain the primary focus of the problem, since it is the shortest distance between two points. Dr. Landry adds that discrimination was still important to the discussion, since perceptions of gender and race influence mobility outcomes.

Commissioner Yaki asks panelists for their thoughts on what the federal government should be doing to enhance the survival and success of minority-owned businesses. Dr. Landry recognizes a high failure rate among all small business and attributes the African-American business failure rate to atrophied or nonexistent informal career networks. Dr. Holzer responds that there are many determinants to the success of African-American-owned businesses, most notably whether the business is family-owned, but does not advocate eliminating racial preferences in federal procurement.

Commissioner Ashley Taylor asks the panelists why the African-American professional class did not subsequently move to the private sector and whether this was a rational decision. He also asked whether other economic and employment decisions made by African-Americans as a group were rational ones. Professor Besharov responds that the decision to remain in government employment was a rational once, citing government pensions and benefits and overall job security as reasons for continued government service. Dr. Holzer cites evidence that the labor market deteriorated in the 1980s for less educated young men, who rationally responded by withdrawing from the labor market. He also states that many of these young men might have turned to participating in the burgeoning crack market, a seemingly rational economic decision in the short-term. Dr. Landry adds that many such young men might have re-entered the booming labor market of the 1990s along similarly rational lines, as the unemployment rate among young African-American males declined during that period.

Commissioner Braceras asks the panelists about the existence and strength of discrimination as a contributing factor to the stagnation. Although Dr. Landry points to test cases that identified discrimination in housing and employment, Dr. Holzer points to limitations of that evidence. For example, the test cases in employment deal with entry to employment and not with promotions, discharges, or other employment actions. Dr. Holzer states that the racial gap in earnings disappears when you examine traditional statistical studies that control for education and test scores. He suggests that there are complex ways in which opportunities are limited for some that are not related to discrimination. Nevertheless, Dr. Landry advocates vigorous enforcement of affirmative action, even for those who have reached the middle class.

Commissioner Braceras expresses concerns that the academic (and later professional) mismatch mentioned by Professor Besharov might increase the perception of discrimination in education and the job market. She asks whether promoting vocational education is an effective way to solve the mismatch problem, given the stigma that some attach to it. Dr. Holzer responds that career academies better integrate strong academics into their curricula when compared to vocational education programs.

Finally, Commissioner Peter Kirsanow asks whether racial preferences at highly selective law schools contributed to the academic mismatch. Dr. Landry attributes this mismatch to school environments and educators' attitudes rooted in racial stereotypes. Commissioner Kirsanow notes that Asian Americans seem to succeed despite these barriers, but Landry attributes their success to parental pressure.

Evidence and Explanation of the Economic Stagnation of the Black Middle Class (Relative to Whites)
Douglas J. Besharov

Since the early 1980s, the black middle class has hardly grown. You may be surprised when I say that, since just about everyone assumes that it is growing. That is because it is growing in absolute numbers (as it is in the general population), but not as a percentage of the black population.

I will trace the reasons why I have come to this conclusion and then offer a partial list of remedies. I will focus on what I consider the most achievable remedy: increasing the college graduation rate of African-Americans by focusing on academic achievement (at all levels of schooling), the mismatch between achievement and school attended, the need for a supportive school culture, and the reform of financial aid formulas.

Slide 1

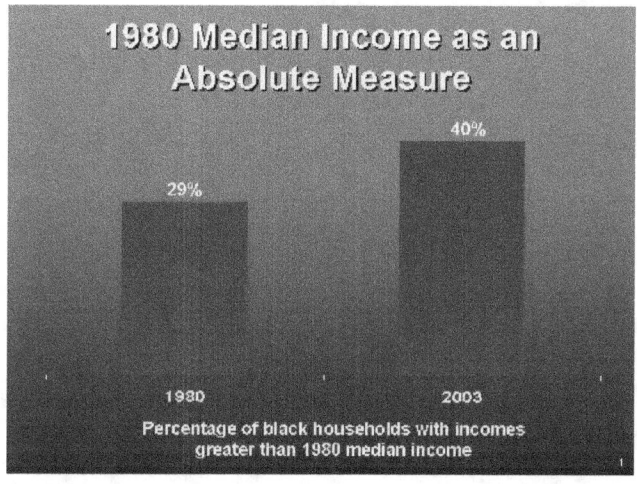

As Slide 1 demonstrates, black economic progress continues. Between 1980 and 2003, the percentage of black households with incomes greater than the 1980 median income of all American households grew by a third, going from about 29 percent to about 40 percent. But that is a comparison with past white incomes, and white incomes have also continued to rise—while African-Americans have not been able to close the gap.

Slide 2

I believe that the best way to see this lack of black progress relative to whites is to examine the percent of African-Americans in different income quintiles. Slide 2 portrays, for the year 2003, the income distribution of all American households, and then indicates both the median income (about $43,000) and the quintile divisions ($0 – about $18,000, $18,000 – $34,000, $34,000 – $54,000, $54,000 – $87,000, and $87,000 and above).

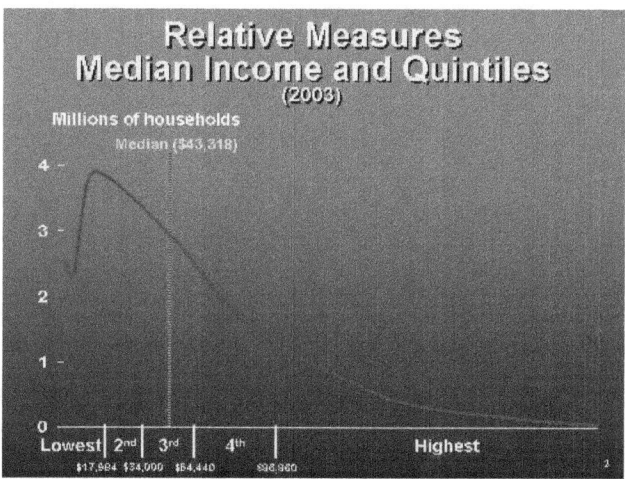

7

Slide 3 shows a number of things about income trends. First, we have added the bottom decile, that is, the bottom 10 percent of incomes. Thus, at the very bottom, African-Americans are twice as likely to be in that group than are whites, and the proportion has hardly changed over the past 45 years.

Slide 3

	Bottom Decile	Bottom Quintile	Top Quintile
1959	22.0%	41.2%	5.9%
1969	18.4%	35.4%	8.1%
1979	20.9%	35.2%	10.1%
1989	21.9%	35.7%	10.3%
1999	19.2%	32.9%	10.4%
2003	19.2%	32.5%	9.8%

Top and Bottom Quintiles/Deciles — Black Households (1959–2003)

Second, at the bottom quintile, there has been progress, with a quarter fewer blacks in that group—although they are still 50 percent more likely to be in that income group than are whites. Third, and also good news, the proportion of African-Americans in the top quintile is about 66 percent higher.

The next three slides show the distribution of households in the middle and top quintiles.

Slide 4

Slide 4 shows the distribution in the middle three quintiles. Looking at it, the distributions seem equal, but that is only because there are so many African Americans in the second quintile, as opposed to the top three.

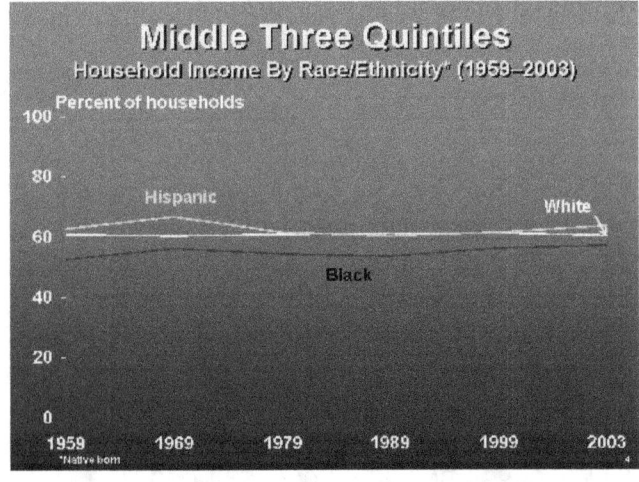

For, as Slides 5 and 6 show, in the top two and the top three quintiles, the lower incomes of African-Americans are quite apparent. Just as importantly, these slides show that—after substantial progress between 1959 and 1979—black incomes relative to white incomes have essentially held constant.

Slide 5

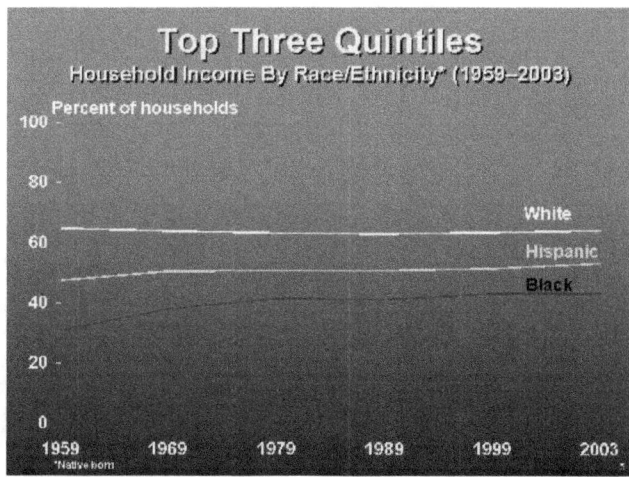

Slide 6

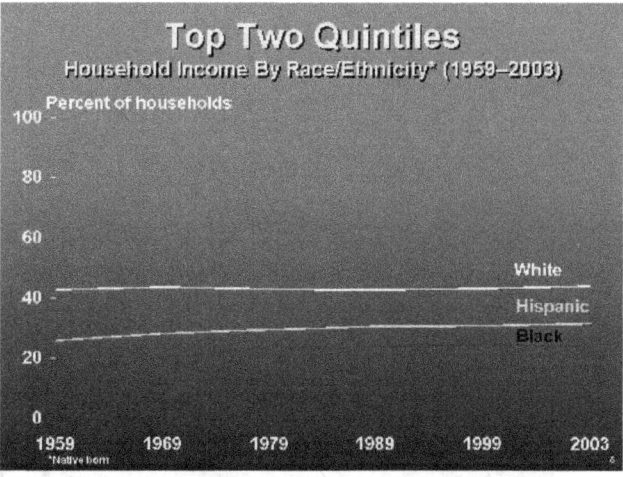

In other words, if one considers the middle class to be, essentially, either the top two or the top three quintiles, the percentage of blacks in the middle class has been stuck at about the same percent since the early 1980s.

Slide 7

Self-Identification of Middle Class Status By Race (1949–1996)		
	Black	White
1949	12%	34%
1956–58	14%	41%
1966–68	15%	46%
1976–78	22%	60%
1988–91	30%	51%
1994	44%	c. 64%
1996	41%	NA

I have added Slide 7 on self-identification as middle class to show the impact of the absolute and relative income measures on African-American attitudes. On the one hand, the continued absolute progress in black incomes is demonstrated by the African-American responses through the 1990s, but the lack of relative progress is mirrored in the higher white self-identification as middle class.

Let me turn now to the most likely culprits. Discrimination, at some level, is surely a factor, although the other factors that I will discuss are just as surely more important.
Family structure helps explain some of the differences between whites and blacks, although there is some argument about the direction of causation. Slide 8 shows how much higher the incomes of married-couple families are compared to female-headed families—of either race. Slide 9 shows that blacks are simply less likely to be in married-couple families.

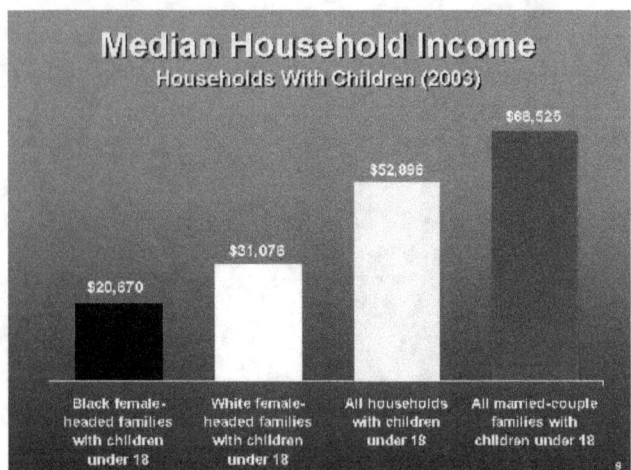

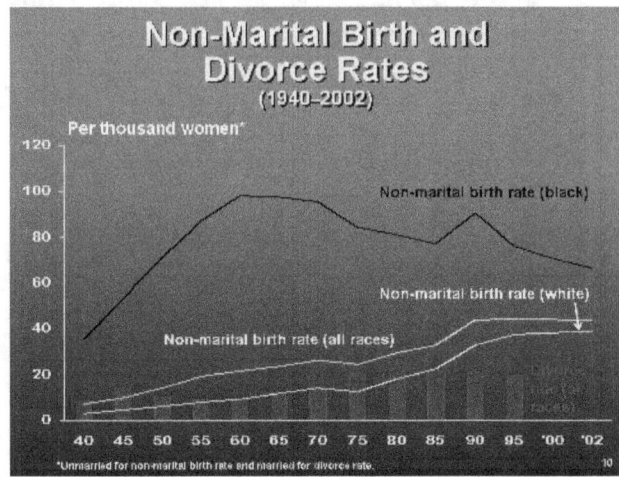

Study after study has shown that black poverty would be much lower if family structures had not weakened beginning in the 1960s. Examining the effect of family structure on child poverty, Isabel Sawhill and Adam Thomas of the Brookings Institution find that "had the proportion of children living in female-headed families remained constant since 1970, the child poverty rate in 1998 would have fallen by 1 percentage point, rather than rising by 3.4 percentage points, relative to the 1970 rate. Thus, the poverty rate is 4.4 percentage points – or 24 percent – lower as a result of assuming marriage patterns similar to those that existed in 1970."[1] Sawhill and Thomas continue, research by Eggebeen and Lichter suggests that, "had there been no changes in family structure between 1960 and 1998, the black child poverty rate in 1998 would have been 28.4 percent rather than 45.6 percent."[2]

Slides 10–12 portray trends in government employment. They are only a minor part of what has happened in the last forty years, but they demonstrate the complexity and changing nature of the factors influencing the incomes of African Americans.

---

[1]*See* Isabel Sawhill and Adam Thomas, *For Richer or for Poorer: Marriage as an Anitpoverty Strategy*, JOURNAL OF POLICY ANALYSIS AND MANAGEMENT, October 8, 2002, at 587-99.
[2]*See id.*

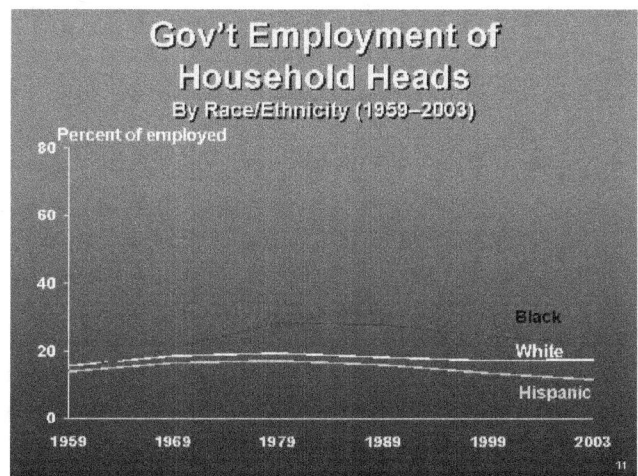

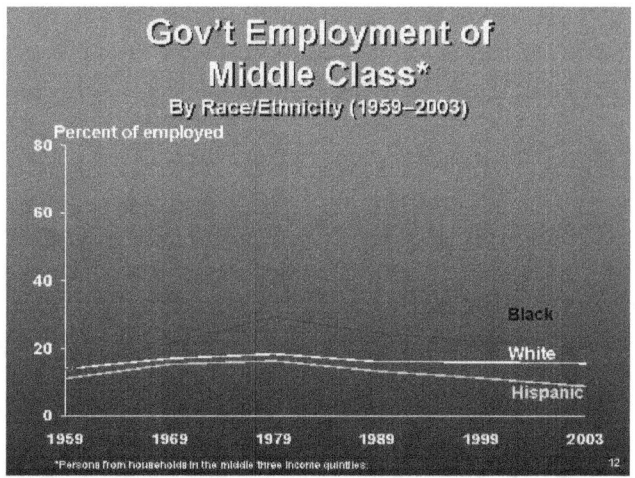

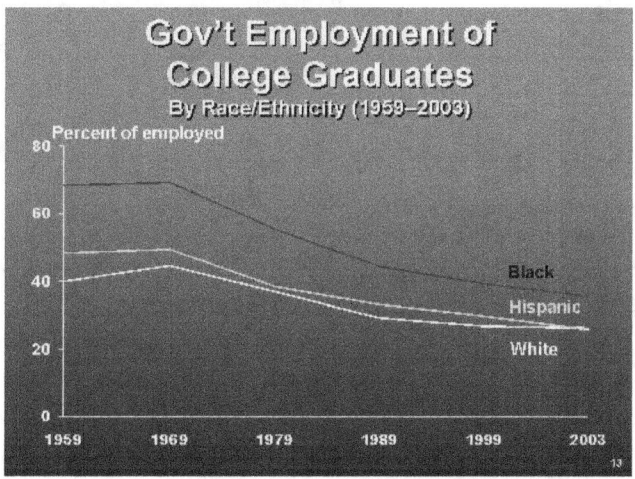

Slide 10 shows two things. First, government employment was an important element of black economic progress from 1959 to 1979. At a time of much greater racial discrimination, government was an important source of jobs for African-Americans. Although government employment has declined, it continues to be higher than that of whites. In fact, after 1979, the higher proportion of blacks working in government may help to explain their income stagnation, as government salaries have not kept up with those in other sectors.

Slide 11 shows that the same story was even more pronounced for the black middle class—with a somewhat higher rise and somewhat larger decline.

Slide 12 quite dramatically shows the declining importance of government employment for all college graduates—blacks, whites, and Hispanics.

This brings me to the crucially important role of education. Economists agree that the U.S. labor market now puts a much greater premium on education and on skills generally than in the past, and that, since the early 1980s, the differences in earnings for workers with different levels of education have grown greatly. That is, all things being equal, since the early 1980s, differences in educational attainment and in work skills generally have resulted in often substantial differences in earnings. Hence, the main proximate cause of the lack of economic progress among African-Americans is the continuing difference in educational attainment between whites and blacks.

In the context of this topic, the black middle class is not growing compared to whites because of high dropout rates in middle and high school, low college attendance rates, and even lower college graduation rates (again compared to whites).

Slide 13

Slide 13 portrays the 30-year rise in high school completion rates, especially for African-Americans (now around 90 percent). (Note that we try to capture current patterns by restricting the analysis to 25- to 29-year-olds.) This slide is somewhat misleading, however, because, since 1992, completion includes those who have obtained a General Education Degree (or GED). Hence, the figures for 1992 and before are probably a better indicator of high school completion, and they suggest much less progress. In addition, sadly, many think that even finishing high school does not

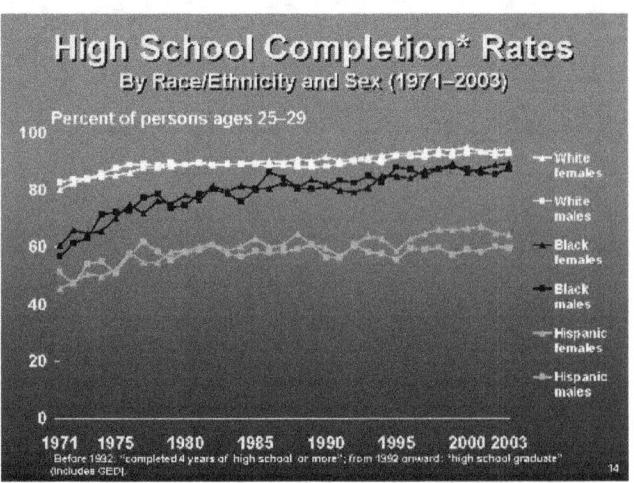

provide the education and skills that it once did, especially in many inner-city schools. (The even lower completion rates for Hispanics are partly a result of large numbers of immigrant children, but they have a similar dampening impact on earnings.)

Slide 14

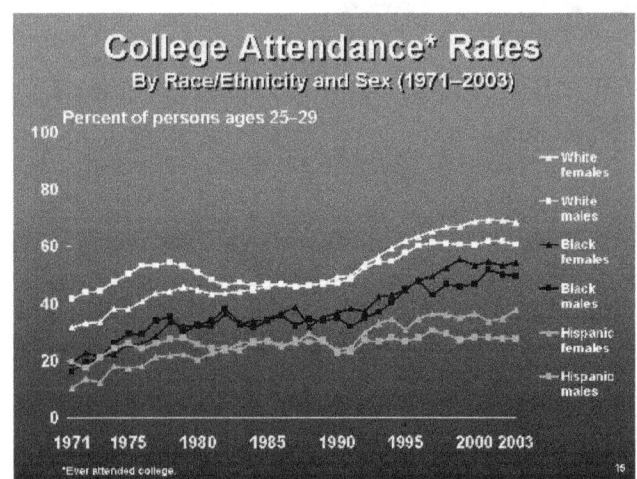

Slide 14 portrays an impressive increase in college attendance rates, for whites and blacks, at least. For instance, the college attendance rate for blacks males increased from about 16 percent in 1971 to about 50 percent in 2003, while the attendance rate for white males went from about 42 percent to about 61 percent.

However, as Slide 15 shows, the graduation rate for African-Americans is not nearly as rosy. Although the rate for African-American males increased from about 7 percent to about 18 percent, that is still only 18 percent compared to the white male graduation rate of 31 percent. (Again, we try to capture current patterns by restricting the analysis to 25- to 29-year-olds.)

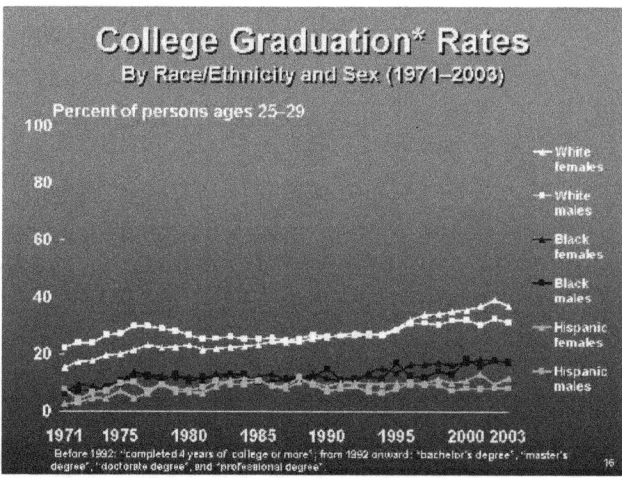

Moreover, the college dropout rate[3] for blacks has actually risen since the 1980s. Let me say that again: Even though the graduation rate has risen for African-Americans, since the 1980s, so has the college dropout rate. Since 1971, the white college dropout rate (as a percentage of those who attend) has decreased from about 50 percent to about 47 percent in 2003. The Hispanic dropout rate has hovered at about 66 percent. But the black dropout rate has increased from about 63 percent in 1971 to about 64 percent in 1980, and then to about 67 percent in 2003.

Everyone, I think, appreciates the tragically low academic achievement of many young people of all races and ethnicities, but with the greatest concentrations among disadvantaged minorities. Why this disappointing level of educational attainment among blacks and Hispanics?

The usual response from the left is to blame discrimination, poverty, and other social ills. The right tends to blame family breakdown and dysfunctional behavior in general. Both sides blame the low quality of the schools many disadvantaged minorities attend. Each of these explanations is to some extent valid, and they all deserve our attention.

But I would like to highlight three other factors that, because they are *institutional (or programmatic),* could be addressed more easily by government or other social institutions than could many other causes.

- *Poor high school counseling*, especially for disadvantaged minorities. I believe the evidence that too many young people go to the wrong college and that the resulting "mismatch" helps explain poor performance in college and high dropout rates in general.[4] If this research is correct, African-American graduation rates would rise if

---

[3]Prior to 1992, the Census Bureau asked respondents to report the highest grade they had attended and whether or not they completed that grade. It was assumed that a person who had completed four years of college had a bachelor's degree; however, students can complete four years of college without receiving a degree and dropout before they do receive one. Since 1992, the questionnaire has asked for the highest grade of school completed or the highest degree obtained. Thus, the dropout rates prior to 1992 could possibly be understated (if there were many dropouts after four years) or, less likely, overstated (if there were many students who obtained a degree in less than four years).

[4]*See* Richard H. Sander, *A Systematic Analysis of Affirmative Action in American Law Schools,* 57 STANFORD LAW REVIEW 367 (2004).

there were a better match between the incoming students' academic achievement and the school's level of academic rigor. Students from disadvantaged families, especially, need better information and advice about where (and how) to apply to college and, if accepted, which schools to attend and how to navigate the student aid process. And, yet, it is just such students who get the least counseling (or inadequate counseling).

- *Unsupportive college cultures* that often seem oblivious to the special challenges faced by young people coming from severely disadvantaged backgrounds. There are clearly right ways and wrong ways to provide support, and this is too important an area to be as unexamined as it is.

- *Financial aid formulas tilted in favor of the middle class.* Many might wish that college was free to all students, or at least to all but the most affluent. But that is not likely in our lifetimes. In the meantime, the limited aid available is inappropriately tilted toward the middle class as a result of the need analysis formula by which aid is determined.

The aid formula disregards all family assets when parental income is less than $49,999 and, regardless of family income, ignores the home equity (however great) in the family's principal residence.[5] (According to Susan Dynarski of Harvard University, those with the highest home values saw the greatest boost to their aid eligibility when this disregard was implemented.[6])

Slide 16

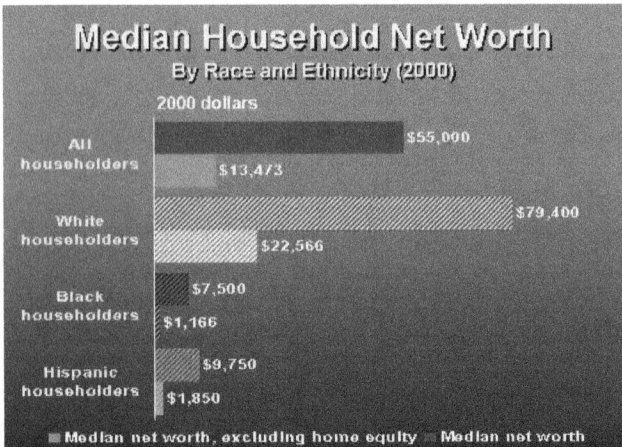

As Slide 16 dramatically shows, disregarding assets and home equity obscures important wealth differences between whites and blacks. This might not be a problem if there were enough funds and more to go around, but there are not. Hence, the effect of these rules is to decrease the amount of aid available for the truly needy.

In fact, grants to low-income students (such as Pell Grants) have failed to keep pace with college costs, and now cover less than half of the cost of tuition, fees, and room and board at the average public four-year college. This forces the lowest-income students to supplement their grants with substantial loans, illustrated by the fact that between 1981–1982 and 2001–2002, the share of all student aid (federal, state, and other) coming in the form of grants fell from 52 percent to 39 percent, while the share in the form of loans rose from 45 percent to 54 percent. In

---

[5]*See* U.S. Department of Education, Office of Federal Student Aid, *The Expected Family Contribution Formula, 2005–2006, available at* http://studentaid.ed.gov/students/attachments/siteresources/EFCFormulaGuide0506.pdf, (last accessed July 12, 2005).
[6]*See* Susan Dynarski, "Loans, Liquidity, and Schooling Decisions," Harvard University, Kennedy School of Government and NBER, Draft at 2 (February 2002), *available at*:
http://ksghome.harvard.edu/~.SDynarski.Academic.Ksg/Dynarski_loans.pdf (last accessed June 23, 2005).

14

addition, unmet need often proves an insurmountable barrier for low-income students. Hence, the current approach to financial aid discourages college attendance and increases the dropout rates of low-income (often minority) students.

As I have described, there are many reasons for the lack of economic progress among blacks relative to whites, including continuing racial discrimination, weaker family structures, higher levels of government employment, and lower levels of educational attainment. One factor limiting the educational attainment of African-Americans is their high college dropout rate, which, I have argued, can probably be ameliorated more easily than the others.

I provided a short list of changes that could increase college completion rates: Before they even leave high school, low-income students need better college counseling, focused on matching them to schools where they have a better chance of succeeding. And because college can be especially stressful for disadvantaged young people, colleges then need to provide supportive environments that address their special needs. Lastly, financial aid formulas should be reformed to end (or at least reduce) the subsidizing of middle-class students at the expense of the lowest-income students. All three measures will require political will, but they do seem to be the most direct way to help more African-Americans finish college.

Expanding the African-American Middle Class: Improving Labor Market
Outcomes
Harry J. Holzer

The data presented by Doug Besharov shows that, despite some progress during the 1990s, the share of African-Americans joining the middle class in the U.S. has stagnated over the past 20 to 30 years. At least some of these trends are closely tied to changes in the labor market for Americans with different levels of educational attainment in that time period.

What opportunities currently exist for blacks in the labor market, and how do these vary with their level of education? What explains the remaining gaps between whites and blacks, and how might the opportunities for blacks be improved over time?

The Data

Table 1 at the conclusion of this chapter presents data on employment rates and median annual earnings for whites and blacks (as well as Hispanics) by gender and educational attainment.[7]

The results suggest four major conclusions:

- Employment and earnings are strongly related to educational attainment for all racial groups.

- The earnings of black men are about 20 to 25 percent lower than those of white men, when compared to those with similar educational attainment; the earnings of black and white women within education groups are somewhat more comparable.

- Employment rates of black men also lag behind those of white men in the same educational categories, especially at lower levels of education.

- The average earnings levels of individual black workers with at least some college education are sufficient to attain middle-class status (requiring at least $30-35,000 of annual income). Those with high school diplomas will usually require two earners in a household to attain that status, unless they can stabilize their employment or attain better non-college jobs.

The strong effects of education on employment and earnings reflect a labor market that puts a much greater premium on education, and skills more broadly, than in the past; indeed, the differences in earnings across education groups have grown greatly over time for all workers in

---

7 The data are computed from the March files of the Current Population Survey over the period 2000-2004, to present a portrait of the current labor market over different points in the recent business cycle.

the U.S.[8] The continuing education gaps between young blacks and whites clearly contribute to earnings gaps between them as well. Blacks continue to drop out of high school in greater numbers than whites, and they enroll and complete college less frequently.[9]

The gaps in earnings between black and white men, even with the same education levels, partly reflect gaps in cognitive skills (as measured by test scores); but other factors are also relevant. A lack of early work experience, persistent discrimination, weak informal networks, and geographic mismatches between jobs and workers contribute to the poor employment experience of black men.[10] Among other effects, these factors limit their access to the better-paying jobs in construction, manufacturing, transportation and some parts of the service sector that will continue to be available to those without college diplomas.[11]

Employment and earnings trends for black females have been much more positive since the 1990's than for males; indeed, the employment of black women is similar to or higher than that of white women in each educational category, while their annual earnings are fairly comparable as well. Only the fact that their educational attainment lags behind that of whites prevents them from achieving parity.

The positive employment trends since the 1990's for less-educated females reflect welfare reform, the growth of work supports (such as the Earned Income Tax Credit) and a strong economy during that time period.[12] In contrast, the continuing decline in work activity for less-educated black men reflects, among other factors, the explosive growth in the number of young men with criminal records in the 1990's, and perhaps the tendency of the child support enforcement system to deter regular employment among low-income black men.[13] These forces

---

8 *See* David Autor & Lawrence Katz, *Changes in the Wage Structure and Earnings Inequality, in* THE HANDBOOK OF LABOR ECONOMICS: VOLUME 3 (O. Ashenfelter and D. Card eds., 1999).

9 *See, e.g,* Thomas Kane, *College Entry by Blacks Since 1970: The Role of College Costs, Family Background, and the Returns to Education,* JOURNAL OF POLITICAL ECONOMY, Vol. 102, No. 5 (1994); CHRIS SWANSON, WHO GRADUATES? WHO DOESN'T? A STATISTICAL PORTRAIT OF PUBLIC HIGH SCHOOL GRADUATION (The Urban Institute 2004).

10 *See, e.g.,* William Johnson & Derek Neal, *Basic Skills and the Black-White Earnings Gap, in* THE BLACK-WHITE TEST SCORE GAP (C. Jencks and M. Phillips eds., Brookings 1998); Harry J. Holzer, *Racial Differences in Labor Market Outcomes Among Men, in* AMERICA BECOMING: RACIAL TRENDS AND THEIR CONSEQUENCES (N. Smelser, W.J. Wilson and F. Mitchell eds., National Academy Press 2000).

11 *See* FREDRIK ANDERSSON, HARRY J. HOLZER & JULIA I. LANE, MOVING UP OR MOVING ON: WHO ADVANCES IN THE LOW-WAGE LABOR MARKET? (Russell Sage Foundation 2005) for evidence on wage differences across sectors of the economy for workers with comparable skills. *See also* PETER EDELMAN, HARRY J. HOLZER & PAUL OFFNER, RECONNECTING DISADVANTAGED YOUNG MEN: IMPROVING EDUCATION AND EMPLOYMENT OUTCOMES (Urban Institute Press, forthcoming 2005) for a discussion of job availability over the next decade for less-educated workers. They argue that, with the coming retirements of Baby Boomers, a great deal of replacement hiring will occur in occupations paying above-average wages that will not require four-year college diplomas, though they will often require significant occupational skills, training and/or work experience.

12 *See* Rebecca Blank & Lucie Schmidt, *Welfare, Work and Wages, in* THE NEW WORLD OF WELFARE (R. Blank and R. Haskins eds., Brookings 2002).

13 *See, e.g.,* Devah Pager, *The Mark of a Criminal Record,* AMERICAN SOCIOLOGICAL REVIEW, Vol. 66 (2003); Harry J. Holzer, Paul Offner & Elaine Sorensen. *Declining Employment of Young Black Men: The Role of Incarceration and Child Support,* JOURNAL OF POLICY ANALYSIS AND MANAGEMENT, Vol. 24, No. 2 (2005). Pager shows that employers are reluctant to hire young men with criminal records, especially young black men. Holzer et al. show that the rising proportion of young black male ex-offenders and non-custodial fathers accounts for much of their employment decline in the 1980's and 1990's.

mostly impact men and women well below the middle-class threshold; but they also will limit the chances of *children* in lower-income black families to enter the middle class in the future.

But, even at higher levels of education, black women have achieved greater parity in earnings and employment with whites than have black men. The fact that young black women are now completing high school and enrolling in college at substantially higher rates than black men also raises concerns about future trends in the growth of the black middle class.[14]

The employment difficulties of black men likely contribute to the growth of female-headed families over the past few decades. Scholars still debate the extent to which the shrinking pool of "marriageable men" contributes to the growth of female headship in the black community, though few doubt that it plays some role. Clearly, the growth of families with only one potential earner in the black community limits the ability of many black families today, and their children tomorrow, to join the middle class.[15]

Policy Implications

The data analysis and discussion above leads me to conclude with the following goals for public policy:

- Improve educational attainment and skill development among blacks at all levels of schooling;
- Improve labor force attachment and access to better jobs, especially among young black men; and
- Raise the number of black families with two adult earners, or at least where fathers contribute to family incomes.

The need to improve educational attainment among blacks exists at all levels of schooling and across many dimensions of skills. Closing the achievement gap in grades K-8 would create dividends in the form of higher graduation rates from high school and higher post-secondary enrollments as well as higher labor market earnings. High school reform efforts might also contribute to closing these gaps.

But it is also important to note that high school reforms should not focus too narrowly on academics or preparation for college, and should also include better options for gaining occupational training and early work experience. Indeed, a focus only on academics and preparation for college could lead to higher dropout rates, while a stronger mix of academic and occupational training along with early work experience will likely induce young people to drop out less frequently. When well designed and implemented, these alternative approaches—

---

14 A gender gap in college attendance and completion exists among whites and Hispanics as well; but, adjusting for the undercount of black men in most survey data because of high incarceration rates, the "gender gap" is greatest among blacks. See Edelman, *supra* note 5. .

15 *See, e.g.,* SARAH MCLANAHAN & GARY SANDEFUR, GROWING UP WITH A SINGLE PARENT: WHAT HELPS, WHAT HURTS (1994); David Ellwood & Christopher Jencks, *Explaining Differences in Family Structure, in* SOCIAL INEQUALITY (K. Neckerman ed., Russell Sage Foundation, 2004); KATHRYN EDIN & MARIA KEFALAS. PROMISES I CAN KEEP: WHY POOR WOMEN PUT MOTHERHOOD BEFORE MARRIAGE (2005).

including Career Academies, School-to-Work programs, and apprenticeships—can clearly lead to higher school completion rates and postsecondary enrollments as well as better employment outcomes for out-of-school youth.16 Greater access to and financial support for lower-income students in higher education, including community colleges as well as four-year institutions, is important as well.

The labor force attachment of young black men can be encouraged not only through improved education, but also through effective post-school training programs for youth and adults. A range of labor market "intermediaries," including private sector "temp agencies" as well as various non-profits and community-based groups, can help bridge the many gaps between employers and prospective black applicants, and improve the access of the latter to better non-college jobs.17

Finally, efforts to strengthen black families and the ties between fathers and children should include not only marriage-promotion efforts, but also "fatherhood" programs and child support reforms. These reforms, and perhaps some earnings supplementation for non-custodial fathers paying child support, could improve the attachment of low-income fathers to their children as well as to the labor market.[18] Special efforts will especially be needed on behalf of those with criminal records.[19] These efforts will not be sufficient to draw most into the middle class, but will perhaps create more positive chances for their children to become future members of the black middle class.

---

16 *See, e.g.,* JAMES KEMPLE, CAREER ACADEMIES: IMPACTS ON LABOR MARKET OUTCOMES AND EDUCATIONAL ATTAINMENT (2004) on Career Academies; DAVID NEUMARK & DAVID AND DONNA ROTHSTEIN, SCHOOL-TO-CAREER PROGRAMS AND TRANSITIONS TO EMPLOYMENT AND HIGHER EDUCATION (National Bureau of Economic Research Working Paper, 2003) on School-to-Work programs more broadly.

17 Examples of effective programs for youth that improve earnings and limit their involvement in crime include the Job Corps and the Youth Service Corps; see Edelman, *supra* note 5. *See also* Andersson, *supra* note 5, for evidence that "temp" agencies, and perhaps intermediaries more broadly, can improve the access of less-skilled workers to better employers and higher-wage jobs.

18 Child support reforms might include changes in how orders are set for low-income men, especially while they are incarcerated, and arrearage "forgiveness" arrangements to encourage the payment of current orders. The Parents Fair Share program was one "fatherhood" effort designed to increase employment and improve father-child contacts, though it was more successful at the latter than the former. Proposals to extend the Earned Income Tax Credit to non-custodial fathers who are paying child support are currently under consideration in the state of New York and Washington, D.C. Another example of a program that shows that earnings supplements can improve the labor force attachment of young black men is the New Hope project in Milwaukee.

19 Efforts to raise labor force activity among those with criminal records could include programs to raise their employment while they are incarcerated; a variety of "reentry" programs, including those that are faith-based; and reviews of state laws that bar employment for ex-offenders in ways that are unrelated to public safety. Since most ex-offenders are also non-custodial fathers with arrearages, the policies described in the previous footnote are especially relevant for this population. See HARRY J. HOLZER, STEVEN RAPHAEL & MICHAEL STOLL, EMPLOYMENT BARRIERS FACING EX-OFFENDERS (Paper presented at 2003 Reentry Roundtable, The Urban Institute).

Table 1. Employment and Earnings by Education, Race and Gender					
		Males		Females	
		% Employed	Median Earnings	% Employed	Median Earnings
Less than high school					
	White	76.3	20984	59.0	12149
	Black	56.0	16081	57.6	10805
	Hispanic	75.6	17671	57.1	11044
High School Diploma					
	White	91.0	31169	78.9	19740
	Black	78.3	24935	75.3	17671
	Hispanic	87.7	24935	76.0	17892
Some College					
	White	93.4	38655	83.0	24000
	Black	86.0	30000	84.6	23896
	Hispanic	91.7	31171	84.1	22641
Bachelor's Degree or Greater					
	White	96.4	57431	86.4	36400
	Black	92.8	44675	92.5	36364
	Hispanic	93.7	46753	87.6	36447
Source: 2000, 2002, 2004 CPS March Supplement (pooled)					
Notes: Only includes persons aged16-54 not enrolled in school and persons born in the United States. Median earnings do not include values less than or equal to 0. All dollars are real 2003 dollars.					

The Black Middle Class: Growth or Decline?
Bart Landry

Let me begin this discussion of the stagnation of the black middle class by briefly describing the sociological approach to class analysis and the definition of class. The concept itself and the idea of measuring inequality by studying classes come from sociology. Within sociology, there are two major traditions of class analysis: one coming from Karl Marx, the other from Max Weber. Together these two scholars are primarily responsible for laying the foundations of class analysis. Both further agreed that the primary class cleavage in industrial societies was between those who owned property and those who did not. By property, they meant the possession and ownership of income producing wealth in industry, finance, and real estate. Everyone else is relatively propertyless, with their most significant wealth being in the form of the house they live in. And while this form of personal wealth does appreciate, it cannot practically be converted into liquid cash as in the sale of stocks or bonds. Therefore, the propertyless—the vast majority of the population— depends on jobs for their livelihood a fact that leads us to the study of income.

When Marx published his major work, CAPITAL, in 1863, the new jobs being created by the millions in the U.S. economy were factory jobs involving manual work. So Marx did not pay any attention to the relatively few non-manual jobs that represented only 6 percent of all occupations by 1870. But when Max Weber wrote about our increasingly stratified society in the 1920s, non-manual, white-collar occupations were growing very rapidly. And in late 19th and early 20th centuries, the contrasting economic position of manual and non-manual jobs was stark. In a period before legalized labor unions, before COLAs, health insurance, and workers compensation, the income gap between manual and non-manual workers drew a sharp contrast between these two groups of workers. Weber referred to the non-manual or white-collar employees as the *middle class*. As a group they stood between the mass of manual factory workers and those who owned the factories and – after the turn of the 19th century – the rapidly increasing large corporations. So within the Weberian tradition of class analysis we draw two major boundaries: the first is still between those who own investment property and those who have to be employed by them, and second between those who have manual or blue-collar jobs and those who have non-manual or white-collar occupations. See Figure 1.

Figure 1: Class Boundaries

PROPERTY – ASSETS
- ❖ STOCKS, BONDS
- ❖ FINANCIAL
- ❖ REAL ESTATE

PROPERTYLESS - JOBS
- ❖ NON-MANUAL (WHITE COLLAR)
- ❖ MANUAL (BLUE COLLAR)

Therefore, within this tradition, we use *occupation* as the indicator of an individual's class position.

Still working within the Weberian tradition, sociologists picture the process in the following 2 stages:

1) During the first part of our life—up to at least 17 or 18 years, and increasingly to ages 21 or 22—we spend our time in school developing the skills that will prepare us individually to enter the labor market.

2) In the second phase of our life, we take these skills and barter or exchange them for a job in the manual or non-manual sector of the labor market. If we attended college, we are able to bargain for one of the positions in the non-manual sector or the middle class. If we did not attend college we find that we are primarily limited to competing in the manual or unskilled service sector and we become working class.

3) The economic resources attached to positions in either of these two sectors determine our living standard.

What are these economic resources? See Figure 2.

Figure 2: Economic Resources Attached to Class Position

CLASS POSITION
- ❖ INCOME
- ❖ JOB MOBILITY
- ❖ JOB SECURITY
- ❖ FRINGE BENEFITS

They include of course *income*. But since the Second World War, there have been others that are increasingly viewed as important as income itself. These are *fringe benefits*, *mobility opportunities*, and *job security*. The importance of these latter resources are borne out by the fierce battles being waged today by many groups of workers, in the airline industry, in the service sector, and wherever workers are unionized and can bargain collectively with management. Having given you a very brief sketch of the sociological approach to class, let me turn to the question at hand.

Is the Middle Class Growing or Declining? Specifically, Is the Black Middle Class Growing or Declining?

Both the white and black middle classes have been growing. When you think of how sociologists define the middle class, you can see that this is not surprising. Except during recessions, the economy expands and more and more jobs are added to both the manual and non-manual sectors. So each continues to grow. Of course, we have to qualify this because part of the manual sector—factory employment—has actually declined, while the unskilled service sector has increased.

But to say that the middle class is growing is a very crude statement, and has to be examined more carefully. You have no doubt been thinking that this division between non-manual and manual is itself fairly broad, especially if used to compare the black and white class structures. So we can make further meaningful divisions within each class: upper and lower middle class strata; and skilled, semi-skilled, and unskilled working class strata. See Figure 3

Figure 3: The Middle Class (White Collar)

UPPER MIDDLE CLASS
❖ MANAGERS & EXECUTIVES
❖ PROFESSIONALS

LOWER MIDDLE CLASS
❖ TECHNICAL
❖ SALES
❖ ADMINISTRATIVE & CLERICAL

I believe these subdivisions make sense to most people and are part of most people's "mental map" of society and the communities in which they live. Using these concepts, let us compare the black and white middle classes starting in 1960.

As I argued in my book, THE NEW BLACK MIDDLE CLASS, for all practical purposes, the black middle class emerged in early 20th century to serve the needs of growing black urban communities. But because of discrimination in both education and the labor market, the black middle class increased by only about 2 percentage points per decade until 1960. The Civil Rights Act of 1964 and the development of affirmative action as an enforcement mechanism resulted in a sea change for the black community. As you can see from Figure 4, the black middle-class grew from 13.4% to 27.9% of employed blacks in the 1960s. With affirmative action in place giving blacks increasing access to colleges and universities, and with enforcement of the Civil Rights Act in employment, the black middle class grew by another 11 percentage points in the 1970s, and continued to grow in the 1980s and 1990s. If you accept the sociological approach to class, the figures speak for themselves. Today, half of all employed blacks hold white collar, middle-class jobs, compared to about 60 percent of white workers. The gap between the *overall* sizes of the black and white middle classes has declined substantially, even though the proportion of blacks in the middle class is still about 30 years behind that of whites.

Figure 4: Growth of the Black & White Middle Classes

	BMC	WMC	D
1960	13.4%	44.1%	-30.7%
1970	27.9%	50.8%	-22.9%
1983	39.0%	56.0%	-17.0%
1990	44.2%	58.6%	-14.4%
2002	51.0%	60.9%	-9.9%

But as I suggested earlier, the division between middle class and working class is a rather crude division. So we need to look more closely at sub-divisions or strata within the middle class. How are black and white middle-class individuals distributed between the upper and lower middle-class segments? As you can see in Figure 5, a higher proportion of whites than blacks are clustered in the upper middle class.

Figure 5: Middle & Lower Middle Classes Compared

YEAR		BLACKS	WHITES		
1983					
	U	35.7 %	43.4 %	7.7 %	
	L	64.3 %	56.6 %		
1990					
	U	36.2 %	46.2 %	10 %	
	L	63.8 %	53.8 %		
2002	U	44.7 %	52.8 %	8.1 %	
	L	55.3 %	47.2 %		

First of all, in 1983 with 43.4 percent and 35.7 percent of whites and blacks concentrated in the upper middle class, there was a gap of 7.7 percentage points. The gap worsened by 1990 before declining again by 2002, but is still standing at about 8.1 percent. This is not trivial. Although blacks have made great strides in climbing the class ladder, they are a considerable distance from parity with whites, especially in the area where it counts most, the upper middle class—and of course the upper class.

The occupations making up the upper middle class are professionals and managers. See Figure 3. These are the occupations that require at least a college degree, are paid the highest salaries, and often are accompanied by supervisory responsibilities. Several recent high profile class action discrimination lawsuits won by women working on Wall Street suggest that upper middle-class occupations are an area of intense discrimination.

Racialized Class Model

How can you explain discrimination in a class society? Earlier I suggested that the mobility process encompasses two stages, the acquisition of skills in the education phase, and the trading of these skills when entering the labor market. Sociologists actually model this process in three stages as you see in Figure 6.

Figure 6: Traditional Class Model of the Mobility Process in the United States

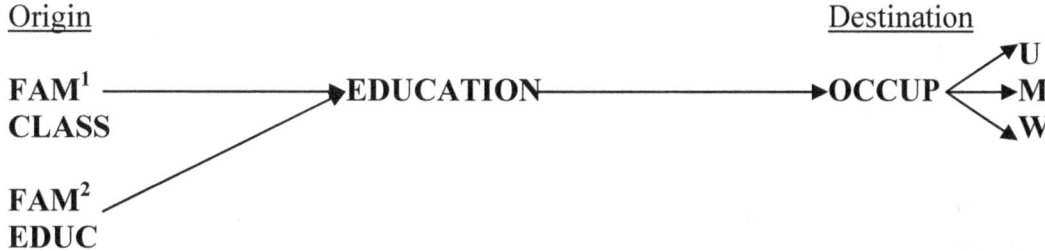

1. **Economic Resources**
2. **Cultural Capital**

On the left hand side you have an individual's *origin* represented by his/her family's class position and level of education. An individual's family's class position represents the economic resources the family has at its disposal to sponsor its children through the educational system. Middle-class families have far more economic resources and therefore have a decided advantage over working-class and poor families, regardless of race. A family's level of education, among other things, includes the cultural capital at their disposal. By cultural capital we refer to the *skills* parents may or may not have acquired. For instance, parents with a college education understand the educational system better, have learned to negotiate with institutions on behalf of their children, and know from experience how to help their children prepare for and apply for college. One of the outcomes is that working-class and poor children are more likely to be put into lower tracks in schools, and as a consequence be less prepared to attend college. In college, they may be handicapped by having attended less rigorous secondary schools. Some recent research suggests a strong correlation between very demanding high school courses and success in college. If children do not attain a college degree, they will not be able to compete for middle-class occupations.

This three-stage process inherently advantages some and disadvantages others, depending upon the class position of their family. But we cannot stop there because we do not have a "pure" class society. We have a class society in which both gender and race influence the mobility process. I earlier alluded to the class action suit some women won on Wall Street over discrimination in promotion and pay. In addition to a suit against Morgan Stanley, they also recently won suits against Wall Mart and Boeing.

The racial model in Figure 7 suggests how African Americans are disadvantaged in the mobility process.

Figure 7: Class/Race Model of the Mobility Process in the Race-Conscious Class System of the United States

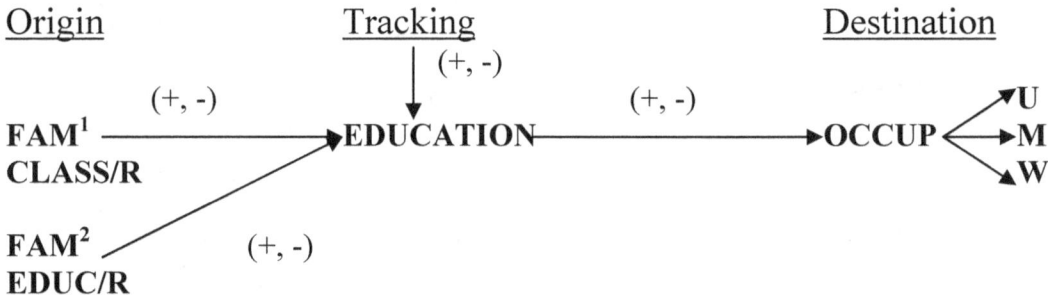

1. **Economic Resources**
2. **Cultural Capital**

I have shown earlier that at the point of family origin, relatively fewer African American than white children can benefit from the resources of upper middle-class parents. Working-class and poor black children are more likely to live in poor areas with inferior schools. But research has shown that even in more affluent areas, white teachers may provide less support to black than white children, and poor and minority children are more likely to be placed in lower tracks that do not prepare them for college. Those who have gained the skills to enter college often cannot attend for lack of financial resources or have to work excessive hours and take out burdensome loans. Once they reach the labor force, like women, they are likely to encounter discrimination in pay and promotion. I should add that this process is *cumulative*. That is each generation begins the process with the financial and educational resources accumulated in the past. Therefore a working-class or poor family has fewer resources than a middle-class family because they were not able to move up the class ladder, and so their children are handicapped by the lesser resources of their parents. That is why schools must have the extra resources to provide them with a quality education that will facilitate their upward mobility. And that is why they need more financial assistance to meet the expenses of a college education.

Conclusion

While I do not agree with Professor Besharov on the definition of the middle class, I agree with him that the growth of the black middle class has been and continues to be impeded by difficulties black families encounter in obtaining quality education for their children at the elementary and secondary levels, and frequently by the lack of resources to support their children in acquiring a college education. Beyond that, the number of gender and race discrimination suits that have been won in areas as diverse as housing, mortgage lending, and employment point to the need for the continued vigorous enforcement of affirmative action, even for those who have reached the middle class.

Statement of Chairman Gerald A. Reynolds on The Stagnation of the Black Middle Class

I can now add Professor Besharov to the list of men and women who have convinced me that one of my fundamental beliefs turns out to be dead wrong. Prior to reviewing his research, I assumed the black middle class was growing percentage-wise. While the black middle class continues to grow in absolute numbers, Professor Besharov's research demonstrates that the percentage of blacks earning their way into the middle class stopped increasing in the mid-1980s. While racial discrimination partially explains the stagnation of the black middle class, Professor Besharov identifies family structure and educational attainment as the primary reasons the black middle class is no longer growing percentage wise. An unsettling truth that we must accept is that many racial disparities cannot be remedied by merely eliminating discrimination. A growing body of research indicates that present day discrimination does not fully explain the existence of racial disparities in income, wealth, and rates of acceptance at selective universities. The research indicates factors, such as family dynamics, market forces and educational attainment, explain a larger portion of these racial disparities.

Race matters, but, in the 21st century, the health of families matters more. Recently Kay Hymowitz, a contributing editor at "City Journal" made the following observation: "[T]he truth is that we are now a two-family nation, separate and unequal—one thriving and intact, and the other struggling, broken and far too often African-American."[20] For quite some time we have known the importance of family in determining a child's opportunities in life. In 1950, the noted black sociologist E. Franklin Frazier stated that:

> As the result of family disorganization a large proportion of Negro children and youth have not undergone the socialization which only the family can provide. The disorganized families have failed to provide for their emotional needs and have not provided the discipline and habits which are necessary for personality development. Because the disorganized family has failed in its function as a socializing agency, it has handicapped the children in their relations to the institutions in the community. Moreover, family disorganization has been partially responsible for a large amount of juvenile delinquency and adult crime among Negroes.[21]

Professor Frazier's mentor, W.E.B duBois, also studied the black family. In 1899, in a seminal work entitled "The Philadelphia Negro," duBois dissected many of the debilitating effects that result from disorganized families. He stated, "[t]he mass of the Negro people must be taught sacredly to guard the home, to make it the centre of social life and moral guardianship." In his capacity as the Assistant Secretary for Policy, Planning and Research at the Department of Labor, the late U.S. Senator Daniel Patrick Moynihan urged the nation to grapple with the fragile state of the black family. Senator Moynihan stated:

---

20 Kay Hymowitz, *The Black Family: 40 Years of Lies*, CITY JOURNAL, Summer 2005.
21 E. Franklin Frazier, *Problems and Needs of Negro Children and Youth Resulting from Family Disorganization*, JOURNAL OF NEGRO EDUCATION, Summer 1960, at 276-77.

At the heart of the deterioration of the fabric of Negro society is the deterioration of the Negro family. It is the fundamental source of the weakness of the Negro community at the present time. There is probably no single fact of Negro American life so little understood by whites. The Negro situation is commonly perceived by whites in terms of the visible manifestation of discrimination and poverty, in part because Negro protest is directed against such obstacles, and in part, no doubt, because these are facts which involve the actions and attitudes of the white community as well. It is more difficult, however, for whites to perceive the effect that three centuries of exploitation have had on the fabric of Negro society itself. Here the consequences of the historic injustices done to Negro Americans are silent and hidden from view. *But here is where the true injury has occurred: unless this damage is repaired, all the effort to end discrimination and poverty and injustice will come to little* (emphasis added).[22]

The societal unit that is the most effective in transferring the skills, values and habits of mind needed for children to thrive in greater society is the family. The black family did not emerge from our nation's history of oppression unscathed. In the 21st century, the greatest legacy of slavery and other forms of oppression is the fragile state of black families. Too many black men and women do not know how to love and live with each other within the institution of marriage. Too many black children are being raised in homes where their fathers are absent. Too many black children have no meaningful relationship with their fathers. The consequences that flow from these fragile families are not "silent and hidden from view." Intractable poverty, crime and poor academic performance are in plain sight for all to see and are closely associated with fragile families. These social ills have robbed generations of blacks of the opportunity to enjoy their citizenship to the fullest degree.

The first phase of the civil rights revolution involved the dismantling of a system of racial apartheid. The second phase will involve strengthening black families. Until we acknowledge the importance of strong families and the likely consequences that result from weak families, it is likely that the racial disparities that surround us, and the stagnation of the growth of the black middle class will become permanent fixtures of our society.

---

22 OFFICE OF POLICY, PLANNING AND RESEARCH, U.S. DEPARTMENT OF LABOR, THE NEGRO FAMILY: THE CASE FOR NATIONAL ACTION 30-31 (1965).

Statement of Commissioner Michael J. Yaki on The Stagnation of the Black Middle Class

It remains a fact that today, more than 50 years after the *Brown* decision, and 40 years after the passage of the landmark Civil Rights and Voting Rights Acts, the African-American community has still not reached the economic parity and equality promised when the legal walls separating them from economic prosperity were torn down. What remains, therefore, is a lesson in what our government and society must continue to do to remedy past discrimination and combat present discrimination.

Unfortunately, our government, particularly the Administration, seeks to simply start from the premise that we are all equal—a noble sentiment in spirit—without accounting for the history of discrimination and the impact that it has had on the African-American community. Yet the mere fact that we have a briefing on the stagnation of the African-American middle class must suggest that barriers—whether they are economic or educational—remain for this community and that equality, while in spirit true, is in fact more elusive than we care to admit.

But we must ask more than the question of the stagnation of the middle class. We must also ask what we can do to lift more out of the middle class and into the highest socioeconomic strata of our society. It is not enough to say we need better guidance counselors in our high schools to facilitate the growth of the African-American middle class. In fact, I become suspicious that the guidance counselors that the Administration and their conservative shock troops talk about are people who will divert African American students into what they believe are more "realistic" or "achievable" colleges and trade schools. Perhaps it is my natural suspicion as a public official, yet it comes on the heels of several "academic" reports claiming that the elite major universities should not engage in affirmative action because it sets unrealistic standards for African-American students. "Guidance counselors" is not an adequate answer to a complex problem with roots over two hundred years old in the history of this country.

I would submit, instead, that it should be our urgent and solemn duty, as a country, to continue such programs and create and innovate new programs that are aimed at enhancing the economic prosperity of African-Americans, particularly African-American business owners. Rather than terminate, as the Administration proposes, we should expand affirmative action programs in federal contracting; rather than weaken, we should reinvigorate Community Reinvestment Act obligations of financial institutions to create better access to capital and credit for the African-American small businesses and to assist in efforts to rebuild neighborhoods through aggressive home lending; and instead of cutting block grant funding for our cities and communities, we need to recognize that we must continue to invest in programs that enrich and expand the opportunities for youth .

Talking about a problem and acting upon a problem are two different things altogether. It is a hallmark of this Administration that it has chosen to do the former, and ignored the policy mandates of the latter.

Speaker Biographies

Douglas Besharov

Douglas Besharov, Professor at the University of Maryland's School of Public Affairs and Senior Scholar at the American Enterprise Institute, was the first director of the U.S. National Center on Child Abuse and Neglect, from 1975 to 1979. With staff in Washington and each of the ten federal regions, the National Center supported research, demonstrations, training, technical assistance, and service projects in all parts of the country. From 1991 to 1992, he served as the administrator of the AEI/White House Working Seminar on Integrated Services for Children and Families, a project designed to improve the delivery of services to disadvantaged children and their families. Besharov's most recent book is Recognizing Child Abuse: A Guide for the Concerned, which is designed to help professionals and laypersons identify and report suspected child abuse. He has written or edited fourteen other books He has also written over 150 articles and contributes regularly to the *Washington Post*, the *Wall Street Journal* and *American Enterprise Magazine*. Besharov estimates that the number of African Americans moving into the middle class has stagnated following dramatic gains in the 1960s and the 1970s.

Harry J. Holzer

Harry Holzer is a public policy professor at the Georgetown Public Policy Institute and holds a PhD in economics from Harvard University. His research has focused primarily on the low-wage labor market, and particularly the problems of minority workers in urban areas. In recent years, he has focused on employer skill needs and hiring practices, as well as the employment problems of less-educated young men. He is currently a senior affiliate of the National Poverty Center at the University of Michigan, a national fellow of the Program on Inequality and Social Policy at Harvard University, and a research affiliate of the Institute for Research on Poverty at the University of Wisconsin at Madison. Previously, he served as chief economist for the U.S. Department of Labor during the Clinton administration, senior fellow at the Urban Institute, and professor of economics at Michigan State University. He has also been a visiting scholar to the Russell Sage Foundation, and a faculty research fellow of the National Bureau of Economic Research.

Bart Landry

Bart Landry is a Professor of Sociology at the University of Maryland, College Park and holds a PhD from Columbia University. In 1987, he published THE NEW BLACK MIDDLE CLASS, which traced the emergence of an African-American middle class in early 20th century and compared its economic position with that of the white middle class in the 1970s and 1980s. Utilizing data he compiled in 1976 as well as 1970 and 1980 census statistics, Landry documented what he labels the "new" African-American middle class and concludes its future faces uncertain growth. He emphasized the widening economic gap between the white and African-American middle class. In his most recent work, BLACK WORKING WIVES: PIONEERS OF THE AMERICAN FAMILY REVOLUTION, Landry explores the impact of middle-class ideologies of black and white womanhood on the development of family systems in the United States. He demonstrates how African-American middle-class wives rejected what he terms "the cult of domesticity" for a three-fold commitment to family, career, and community. His current research centers on the New Economy and the globalization of class.

www.ingramcontent.com/pod-product-compliance
Lightning Source LLC
Chambersburg PA
CBHW080735290526
45790CB00008B/3199